The Little Big Car

Written by Sue James

Illustrated by Josh Manges

© Sue James 2017 All Rights Reserved

Published in USA by Sue James

Dedicated to Eve, who is a LITTLE girl with BIG dreams.

I love you so.

Emma, Happy Counting! Sue Tann May 2018

Acknowledgements
This book was made possible because of the collaborative efforts of many talented people including, our editor, Nora Dickey, Illustrator, Josh Manges, Jessica Brown, my daughter, and the children in Miss Sue's Child Care.

Teach Your Child to Count Using this Book

As you and your child explore The Little Big Car, encourage your child to say aloud the number on each page. Then, actually touch the farm animal and have your child count them. Example: One cow, then have your child touch the cow and count, ONE. Two horses, have your child touch each horse and count ONE, TWO. Touching each animal while counting aloud reinforces the concept of one-to-one correspondence. Don't worry if they make a mistake or pronounce a number wrong, that's fine. Just keep counting the animals as the story unfolds. With practice, your child will eventually be able to count aloud and apply this technique without your help.

Children love repetition and that is key to learning. Be consistent on each reading, counting the animals with your child and say the numbers out loud. After reading The Little Big Car a few times, your child will be able to count making them confident and you will be proud of this accomplishment.

One day, a very big lady got out of a little red car. "That is a very cute little car," I told her.
"Well, this is really a very big car!" she said in a booming voice.

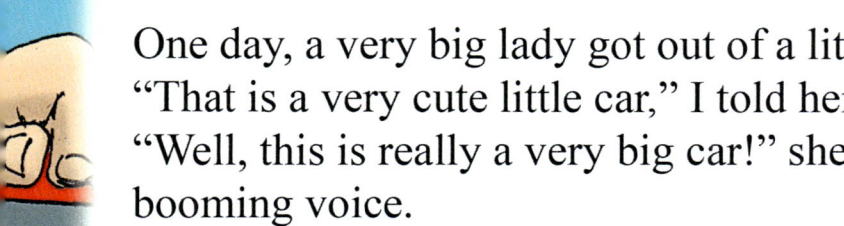

"We have a farm and when the tractor broke down, I put ONE cow in this little car. Down the road we went."

"Did you and the pigs fly down the road?" I giggled.

"Sheer joy!" I remarked wearing a fleece jacket.

"Were they six geese-a-laying?" I said smiling at her.

"Also, I put SEVEN donkeys in this little car. Down the road we went."

"Dog gone lucky dogs," I howled.

"Nine cats with nine lives?" I asked.

"You must work on that farm around the cluck!" I asked her chick to chick.

And then, she walked away.

About the Author

   Sue James has been a child care provider for over seventeen years. Often, she tells stories to help the children in her care understand their world. She lives in Waynesboro, Pennsylvania with her daughter, husband and three cats. This is her second children's book.

About the Illustrator

When not working full-time with at-risk youth or drawing pictures, Josh can most often be found galavanting off on some hare-brained adventure with his children.

Made in the USA
San Bernardino, CA
05 September 2017